The Prestige
West Yorks....

John Banks
Photography by G H F Atkins

© **2001 J M Banks & G H F Atkins**

ISBN 1 898432 29 5

Cover: West Yorkshire's Bristol RELL6G **1287** (**BWU552H**), with 53-seat Eastern Coach Works body, was typical of the fleet in the nineteen-seventies. It was at Harrogate in September 1975.

Rear cover: A bargain two-pennorth. Twopence (less than one new penny) bought this 216-page West Yorkshire timetable, complete with fold-out map and abridged list of local train departures, in October 1936. *(West Yorkshire Information Service)*

Title page: The majestic York Minster, long before the fire and subsequent rebuilding, forms a mighty backcloth for **Y244** (**WW7111**), a Tilling-Stevens B10A2 31-seater of 1928 with a 1936 Bristol body.

Opposite page: The creation of the National Bus Company was bound to bring in its wake profound changes. Not the least of these was in the matter of liveries. Long-distance coaches became all-white but for dual-purpose vehicles a rather more imaginative scheme of white above the waistrail and poppy-red below was adopted. West Yorkshire's **1066** (**7937WU**), a 1960 Bristol MW6G 39-seater, was at Leeds Road, Harrogate in September 1973, not long after receiving its new livery.

Below: The National Bus Company constituents were suddenly allies instead of competitors after 1st January 1969. One of the results was the use of the BET design of windscreen on former Tilling Eastern Coach Works-bodied vehicles. This trio of West Yorkshire Bristol REs includes two such redesigned examples, alongside one of the earlier, flat-fronted, Tilling-designed, bodies. The photograph was taken at Otley bus station in September 1976.

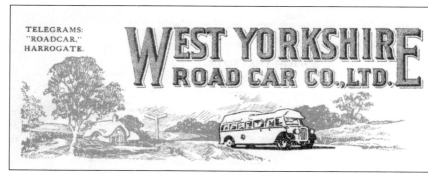

TELEGRAMS:
"ROADCAR."
HARROGATE.

WEST YORKSHIRE ROAD CAR CO., LTD.

TELEPHONE:
HARROGATE 6061
4 LINES.

Head Office :
East Parade,
HARROGATE.

INTRODUCTION

Readers of earlier volumes in this series will have realised that the writer was born and spent his formative years in the city of Kingston-upon-Hull and that certain operators - Hull Corporation, East Yorkshire, United - were very familiar to him. Others - Yorkshire Traction, Lincolnshire and Yorkshire Woollen to name but three - were rather more mysterious.

The West Yorkshire Road Car Company Limited fell between the two extremes. Apart from any other consideration, West Yorkshire half-cab Bristol single-deckers appeared in Hull's Paragon coach station on the jointly worked (with East Yorkshire) service 46 from Leeds via York and Pocklington. Then there were the frequent Sunday visits to Scarborough during youthful summers when the Company's vehicles were seen mingling with those of United and East Yorkshire. It was the sight of West Yorkshire and United side by side in Scarborough that convinced a certain otherwise ill-informed stripling that the two operators had much in common although he had at that stage no inkling of the name Tilling and its connotations.

York was another fairly regular pilgrimage destination on those far-off weekends. Some of the buses there had the fleetname "York-West Yorkshire" and - again - it was to be some years before the young enthusiast came to understand the reason for that.

Some years after these early experiences the writer made the acquaintance of the Nottingham-based photographer G H F Atkins. That was more than three decades ago and the intervening years have afforded the writer the privilege of having become a friend of Geoffrey Atkins and to have seen his peerless collection of transport photographs.

It will be evident to regular readers of this series of books that the Atkins Collection is virtually without equal. Geoffrey was born in 1912, took his first bus photograph in 1927 and is still taking them seven and a half decades later.

Geoffrey Atkins built up his collection painstakingly in order to provide a visual record of bodywork. There are as many directions of interest, almost, as there are enthusiasts. One will concentrate on vehicles and reck little or nothing of how the vehicles earned their living, another interests himself in the services operated with no more than a passing glance at what was working the route. Yet others find company history and premises used to be of abiding interest. The art of the coachbuilder is Geoffrey's principal interest: the services being operated and, to some extent, the locations, are of secondary interest.

Like many another impecunious young enthusiast, Geoffrey found in his youth that he would perforce have to be selective, for money for film, processing and travelling to take the photographs was at a premium. Thus he often had to forego pictures of many vehicle types when the allowance of film for the day was used up. He has never been a motor-vehicle owner and is thus restricted, if that is the word for the journeyings of a transport photographer, to using public transport.

Back home after a day out, or a summer holiday in Scarborough or Llandudno, the processing and printing would be done on equipment carefully chosen for the job and the resulting postcards filed away for future enjoyment. There was no thought of publication then, although many GHFA pictures have appeared in various books and periodicals in recent times. This series of books, which arose out of a tentative suggestion that perhaps Geoffrey's London Transport material might make a small book (it did indeed, as *Prestige Series* number six), is the first to offer enthusiasts an in-depth look at Geoffrey's work produced in nine consecutive decades: a photographic career surely without equal.

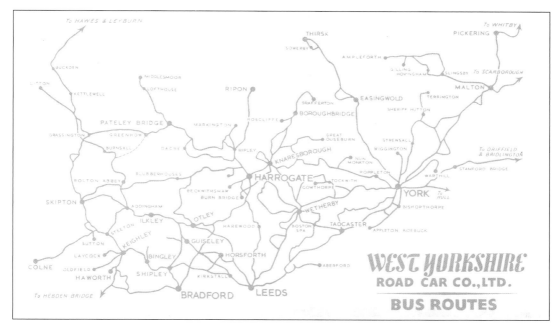

Most operators printed maps in their timetables and most not unnaturally placed their headquarters town in the middle of the map. Here the world revolves around Harrogate in a map used in the Company's timetable issued on the 6th March 1955. The major West Riding cities can be seen to be at the very edge of West Yorkshire's territory. (West Yorkshire Information Service)

The very earliest GHFA West Yorkshire photographs are from 1928 and 1929 and our coverage extends to the late 1980s.

As always in this series of books I have to acknowledge the willing and expert help of my friends Ron Maybray and Philip Battersby. Philip's contribution, indeed, is so interesting that I have included it complete as the reminiscence reproduced below.

Brian Horner and David and Mary Shaw have kindly read the proofs and I must record with grateful thanks the generous and unstinting assistance given by John Gill of the West Yorkshire Information Service, who has not only read and checked the captions but has provided details from his expert knowledge of the Company that the writer - unaided - would have been unable to include. John has also supplied the timetables, map and other company ephemera illustrated in these introductory pages and on the back cover.

Readers are reminded that, as always with the *Prestige Series* albums, no claim is made that either a history of the Company or a fleet list is being offered.

John Banks
Romiley, Cheshire
December 2000

WEST YORKSHIRE - A REMINISCENCE

Each reader will have his own immediate image of "West Yorkshire". It will depend on several things. First, whether he is a native of the area or an outsider; second, whether his formative years were before, during or after the formation of the Passenger Transport Authorities in 1969 and the monumental reorganisation of English local government that took place in 1974; and third, whether he views the title as the name of a bus operator or the description of a territory. In compiling this book, the authors and publishers are quite clear; we are presenting you with a survey of the West Yorkshire Road Car Company through the superb pictures of Geoffrey Atkins. This survey ranges across the Company's history from its formation in 1928 to its delightful but all too brief classic Tilling-liveried swansong after the 1986 deregulation.

The Company's title, like those of many others, and the tramway companies before them, was a grandiose proclamation which did not quite match the reality. The geographical West Riding of Yorkshire is a vast area, but the Company's position as the established territorial operator embraced only Harrogate, Leeds, York, Bradford, Keighley and Skipton. Even there, the territory was only to the north of a line through

From the days of bobs, tanners and threepenny bits, a selection of WYRCC Bell Punch tickets.

Top row: Standard West Yorkshire tickets in use until 1949/50. These were clipped in the lower half for single fares and in the upper for returns.

Bottom row left: A York-West Yorkshire 1d. ticket, standard except for the overprinted "Y".

Bottom row centre & right: Keighley-West Yorkshire examples were the same colours as standard tickets but overprinted "C" for the Keighley-Colne route or with blue stripes on all other routes. (WYIS)

the centres of Leeds and Bradford. True, the West Yorkshire company reached virtually all parts of the West Riding, but much of this was on joint long distance services. These took the company to Wakefield, Barnsley, Doncaster, Sheffield, Dewsbury, Huddersfield and Halifax (but apparently not Rotherham), en route principally to Birmingham, London, Manchester and Liverpool.

A sense of confusion was created when the West Yorkshire PTE took over the more northerly municipal operators in the West Riding. This was because there were now two West Yorkshire bus operators, and it became necessary to distinguish the long established West Yorkshire Road Car Company from the new West Yorkshire PTE. The latter used the fleetname "Metro", which in one sense was a help, but it was an uninspired choice that implied the Paris underground and, later, an Austin car and a thousand and one other things.

The distinctiveness of the Road Car Company was further eroded when a new administrative county of West Yorkshire was created in 1974, and among many anomalies the West Yorkshire company's headquarters at Harrogate were placed within the territory of a new North Yorkshire authority. As the PTE got to grips with its appointed task of coordinating all the services in its territory, large segments of the Road Car Company's operation were either taken over by the PTE or run on its behalf with vehicles painted in its livery. The visible West Yorkshire company of yore was in effect reduced to the operations at Harrogate, York and Keighley. Nowadays the Blazefield Group operating Harrogate & District and Keighley & District is the direct successor, and the York services are in the hands of First York and of Yorkshire Coastliner.

If the reader is a native of the area and these events occurred during his adult life, all the above will seem self evident. If, like the present writer, he comes to the West Yorkshire company from outside, he will begin with odd pieces of a jigsaw and not much idea of how to piece them together. My first sight of West Yorkshire came circa 1952 when I was 11. A friend whose parents had a car invited me to join them on a day out from Bishop Auckland to York. All that I can remember of the day is the friend saying to me, slightly mischievously, *"Look at all those United buses"*. They were of course the vehicles of the York-West Yorkshire joint committee, operated in the city by West Yorkshire in conjunction with York Corporation. Their immediate appearance was indeed very similar to the United buses we knew in County Durham, mostly standard Tilling types on Bristol chassis and/or with Eastern Coach Works bodies, painted in Tilling red and cream with black lining and gold lettering. It was the differences that made the most impression - the thinner style of lettering used in the fleetname, and similarly on the destination blinds. The latter were almost an upper case version of what is usually called spidery writing, and it was not as easy to read as the thick block lettering used by United - but they could get far more letters on to the screen. In addition, although the vehicles themselves were very similar, particularly with standard postwar models, they were not identical. To take a case in point, each company had the prewar Bristol L5G with ECW body, but each had its own body styles not found quite the same anywhere else.

A couple of years later this same friend joined me for what must have been my first ever day of bus riding just for the sake of it. We went south to Ripon, then Harrogate, and then even to Leeds. I was perhaps aged 13 or 14 at this stage, and it was a significant adventure. It was probably at this time that I noticed the West Yorkshire fleet numbers, in classes reminiscent of United's but not the same. What we in United territory knew as a BG they called an SG or

An imaginative montage, part drawing and part photograph, gives a "through the windscreen" view for the front cover of the West Yorkshire timetable issued on 28th September 1958. The back cover exhorted one to "see Yorkshire by bus" with illustrated descriptions of a number of places served by the Company's buses and coaches. (West Yorkshire Information Service)

even an SGL, and what we called a BBL was a DB or a DBW. It was many years before I learned that this sort of similarity was due to the movement of senior staff from one company to another. To avoid confusion, especially between vehicles of neighbouring operators, the similarity also included the sort of differences I have indicated, although in the case of W Alexander and Coras Iompair Eireann many of the classifications (which were not initial letters of makes or types) were exactly the same. The

West Yorkshire fleet numbers were also applied to the vehicles in slightly different positions from those used at that time by United. It was doubtless no coincidence that the cabside and bonnetside positions for fleetnumbers had been used for all United vehicles in the 1923-35 period, and had become established in the minds of the brothers E C and H N Tuff as the only right positions for fleet numbers!

A family move to Middlesbrough brought me into daily contact with West Yorkshire, which reached the town on the Tyne-Tees-Mersey services described in Number Seven in this *Prestige Series* of books. Travel on this service gave a strong impression of West Yorkshire's activities. Their local services were reached at Ripon railway station, whence they operated jointly with United to Harrogate. Upon reaching Harrogate, West Yorkshire buses were everywhere, as befitted their home town. The presence in the Company's bus station of the independent Samuel Ledgard Ltd added further interest, with almost an air of the spider's invitation to the fly, Ledgard being eventually taken over by West Yorkshire in 1967. The journey into Leeds brought the observer into what seemed much more serious West Yorkshire territory. Here the Company owned a depot in Roseville Road, and two bus stations - Vicar Lane and Wellington Street. The latter was for long distance services and hosted a large variety of joint operators. Apart from the West Riding company's minuscule premises in New York Street, no other company had its own bus station in the city, although Wallace Arnold had a coach station. The rest used street stances or the vast municipal Central Bus Station which was also on New York Street. West Yorkshire's workings out of Leeds were of course out-of-town services, the city services being held by the trams and buses of Leeds Corporation. The main roads to Ilkley, Harrogate, Wetherby and York were all held by West Yorkshire, and took the passenger through lush rolling countryside and delightful villages offering a prosperous appearance. The York road had the Company's buses on the long journeys to the coast, with a comprehensive range of services taking West Riding folk to Malton, Whitby, Scarborough, Bridlington and Hull, with some joint working involving East Yorkshire and United.

Visits to Bradford were first prompted by the launch of that city's restored tramcar No. 104 in 1958, and a West Yorkshire Lodekka carried me on one of the two services from Harrogate. In the city I found that West Yorkshire owned the bus station here too, and a depot. As in Leeds, the city services were the province of the municipality, in this case an eminently successful trolleybus stronghold. The Company's out-of-town services were particularly notable to the north west, reaching Keighley where an intensive local network was provided. This was operated under the title of Keighley-West Yorkshire through a jointly owned company with the Corporation. Beyond Keighley the road to Skipton took the Company's buses into the challenging but beautiful Pennine Hills. Here you found a very different West Yorkshire, with sparse services to remote Dales villages, depots at Skipton, Grassington and Pateley Bridge, and even market services to Hawes and Leyburn. The whole was connected back to its origins by the remarkable 76 service, worked by Lodekkas in the 1950s. This operated east from Skipton to Ilkley, Otley, Harrogate, Wetherby and Tadcaster, a 40-mile journey taking 2 hours 25 minutes.

There were other outposts where you would come across West Yorkshire buses, such as Colne and Ampleforth, reached by buses from Keighley and Malton depots respectively. Indeed, not only Colne but other large chunks of Lancashire were traversed by West Yorkshire coaches and buses, bound for Liverpool, Blackpool and Morecambe. All these things form part of this writer's memories, and find vivid expression in the wonderful photographs in the following pages. But perhaps the quintessential memory is of West Yorkshire at speed. On one occasion on a journey from Liverpool to Middlesbrough, the driver took an unscheduled tea break at Oldham, a fast run from Manchester being followed by *"Right, twenty minutes here"*. The bus was a Bristol LWL6B saloon. The clock showed calibration up to 50 mph, but on the road downhill between Dewsbury and Leeds the needle passed 50 and went off the scale, with the bus vibrating rather alarmingly. However, all was well! On another occasion a journey north from Leeds on an LS5G saw 62mph reached down Harewood bank with, again, the sort of control that found us comfortably rounding the corner at the end. This is the West Yorkshire I like to remember, and I hope that these pictures bring it alive for you, as they have done for me.

Philip Battersby
Middlesbrough
November 2000.

Above: West Yorkshire's original departure point in Eastborough, Scarborough in June 1929 was host to No. **214 (WW4257)**, a 31-seat Tilling-bodied TSM B10A. The bus was little more than a year old and was one of a batch of 28 that, when new, had been fitted with single-line roller destination blinds. In this view the roller blind had been replaced by "Bible" indicators of the original style with vertical hinges to turn the sheets.

Below: Number **718 (WX8977)** was a 1932 TSM B49A7, one of 30 bodied by Eastern Counties as 34-seaters. These were the last TSMs delivered to the Company. A York depot allocation, it had come in to Scarborough from Leeds via York and Malton. Behind No. 718 can be seen a 1930 TSM B10A2, No. **273 (WX2129)**. This Roe-bodied 30-seater was one of 40, variously bodied by Tilling (10), Roe (10) and United (20). In June 1935 it had arrived in Scarborough on the marathon stage service from Skipton via Ilkley, Otley, Harrogate and York.

An RAC patrolman directs the driver of No. **151 (WW4278)** in Weston Super Mare in June 1928. One of eight Tilling-bodied TSM B10B *chars-à-bancs* dating from 1928, the vehicle was on a Keighley to the Cornish Riviera tour, an unusual operation for West Yorkshire at that date.

Above: Number **502 (WW9049)**, a 1929 Roe-bodied Leyland Tiger TS1, was equipped with coach seating and luggage racks, thus fitting it for use on express work. In this August 1929 view at Huntingdon Street, Nottingham, the brand new vehicle was operating the Birmingham to Harrogate service.

Below: Fifteen Leyland TS1s were delivered in 1931. Five were bodied by United and the remainder, including No. **523 (WX5914)**, seen in Nottingham in August 1933, by Roe. All were front-entrance 30-seaters. The original method of illuminating the "Bible" indicators, as on No. 502 *(above)*, was by bulbs in a trough at the bottom of the indicator. The bulbs frequently failed because of rainwater filling the trough and the layout was soon changed, as seen on No. 523, by positioning lamps at either side of the indicator.

In 1936, eighteen 1929-31 Leyland TS1 Tigers were stylishly rebodied as 29-seat coaches by Eastern Counties. The original livery is shown *(above)* on No. **564** (**WX2103**) in an August 1936 photograph. Several were quickly repainted cream with red relief as shown *(<<< opposite page)* on No. **561** (**WW9794**), photographed in June 1936, whilst some became red to the waistline and cream above, a style also seen on the AEC Regal illustrated below. This AEC came from Corcoran Bros (Ideal), Tadcaster in November 1933, an acquisition which eliminated competition on the Leeds-York-Scarborough route. Of ten Regals acquired, the six most modern were rebodied as 28-seat coaches by Eastern Counties in 1935. With fleet numbers 688 - 693, all were allocated to Harrogate depot after rebodying. They were put into store from 1939 to 1946 and lasted in service thereafter until 1950. It is not known which one of the six features in this August 1935 view. All three pictures were taken at Huntingdon Street, Nottingham.

Number **544** (**YG56**), seen at Nottingham in August 1935, was a Leyland Tiger TS4 with Eastern Counties 28-seat coachwork, one of a batch of six new in 1932. It was a Harrogate allocation until November 1933 when it was transferred to Leeds. It survived until September 1939.

Six more Eastern Counties-bodied 28-seat TS4 Tigers came in 1933. They were delivered in standard half and half red and cream colours but were soon repainted in "streamlined" livery as shown by No. **549 (YG2194)**, photographed at Nottingham in August 1937. The batch was repainted in service bus livery after the war.

15

Above: Between 1933 and 1935 West Yorkshire's "standard" single-decker was the Dennis Lancet I with Eastern Counties 34-seat front-entrance bodywork. Number **802** (**YG3041**) was the first of 42 delivered in 1933. It was allocated to Harrogate until transferred to Bradford in April 1934. It was in Nottingham, operating as an express duplicate to Birmingham, in August 1933.

Below: Thirteen Dennis Aces joined the West Yorkshire fleet in the 1930s. YG5740 was new in 1934 as fleet number 118. It had Eastern Counties 20-seat bodywork and was renumbered 606 in 1937. During the war six Aces were converted for use as depot vans, including this one, which became **1013** when the service stock was renumbered in 1948 in a series from 1001 upwards. 1013 was the Leeds depot van and it is seen in Vicar Lane, Leeds in August 1949 running on trade plates **476C**.

From 1935 West Yorkshire standardised on Bristol chassis with Eastern Counties (later Eastern Coach Works) bodies. The first Bristol single-deckers were JO5G 32-seaters, new in 1935. Number **911 (YG9006)** *(above)* was one of the first batch of 20. It was photographed at Chester Street bus station, Bradford in September 1936 when working the Bradford to Baildon service. The destination had by now moved to the bottom of the layout on the "Bible" indicator. Number **921 (AWW161)** *(below)* was the first of the second batch of 20 JO5Gs, all of which entered service on 1st January 1936. It was at Valley Bridge bus station, Scarborough in June 1937. This vehicle was a Leeds depot allocation for the whole of its life until withdrawal in September 1951. A smaller fleetname transfer was introduced in 1937, as seen on 921. The bus also has the later, horizontally hinged style of "Bible" indicator. Service numbers were introduced in 1936 and were shown in red to the left of the intermediate points.

The postwar livery and condition of the Bristol Js is shown in this view of No. **953** (**AWX805**) at Vicar Lane bus station, Leeds in August 1949. The bus was withdrawn in October 1951.

The first Bristol double-deckers were of the GO5G type. Fifteen were ordered for 1935 delivery for use in the York-West Yorkshire Joint Committee tramway replacement programme. Fleet number **Y327 (AWW32)**, at York railway station in June 1937, shows the later livery style. The GO5G across the road is in one of the earlier styles and also shows the rear destination board on the cream band. The Leyland TD1 behind AWW32 was one of 12 transferred from WY to YWY, also for tramway replacement work, in 1935.

Above: Nineteen-thirty-five also saw the arrival, in the main West Yorkshire fleet, of a batch of 13 GO5Gs with 53-seat lowbridge bodywork by Eastern Counties. In this September 1936 view at Chester Street bus station, Bradford, No. **313 (YG8993)** was on the busy route 67 to Keighley, one of West Yorkshire's most profitable services.

Below: Here is the marathon route 46 from Hull to Leeds, jointly operated with East Yorkshire, mentioned in the introduction. This view, however, was taken before the writer was born. In June 1937, No. **977 (BWT772)**, a brand new Bristol JO5G with 32-seat Eastern Coach Works service bus bodywork, is passing through York on the way to Leeds. This is probably the 9.25am departure from Hull, scheduled to pass the point in the picture at about 11.20am and arrive in Leeds at 12.30pm.

Six Bristol L6Gs with Eastern Coach Works 30-seat coach bodies were delivered in November 1939, two months after the outbreak of war. During a rebuilding programme of 1952 they were modified in appearance at the front with redesigned windscreens and the more modern, lower-mounted PV2 radiator. At the same time they were repainted in the standard cream coach livery as on No. **641** (**DWU139**) *(above)*, seen at Nottingham very soon after the rebuilding work. During the winter of 1953/54 all six were repainted red with cream relief and became EG7 - 12 in the 1954 renumbering scheme (rather than CG1 - 6 as originally intended). **EG12** (**DWU143**) *(below)* shows off the red livery at Derby bus station in August 1955. It was working the Coventry to Newcastle "Fawdon" service (see *Prestige Series No. 7 "Tyne-Tees-Mersey"*). These coaches carried black-on-white destination blinds from new in 1939 until withdrawal in 1957 and never had "Bible" indicators.

After receiving ten Bristol L6Bs with Eastern Coach Works dual-purpose 31-seat bodies in 1948, six L5Gs with identical coachwork were delivered in 1949 as fleet numbers 249 - 254. Number **250 (GWX135)** with its Gardner 5-cylinder engine *(above and <<< opposite page)* would have provided plenty of noise and vibration but not much performance on the run to London in September 1949. The location was Grantham's Old Bus Station. The ECW bodywork, though externally merely an enhanced version of the standard service bus body, was undeniably attractive (the basic design was among the more aesthetically pleasing of that or any other era - one of the classics indeed) and we include *(below)* an offside-front view of No. **252 (GWX137)** at Wellington Street coach station, Leeds in August 1949. It was operating on the Scarborough to Keighley express service - itself no mean test for five-cylinder Gardner power, perhaps more so than the straight trunk roads to the Capital.

The first postwar coaches in the West Yorkshire fleet were four Duple-bodied Bedford OBs, fleet numbers 646 - 649, of which No. **646 (FWW596)** is pictured at Northway bus station, Scarborough in July 1950. It was in the original livery of cream and red with maroon wings. All four were subsequently repainted in the cream coach livery and No. 646 later achieved some celebrity as the City of York tour coach.

Above: Fifty Bristol L5Gs with Eastern Coach Works 35-seat rear-entrance bodies entered service between 1946 and 1950. The York-West Yorkshire fleet received ten (Y236 - 245, later YSG121 - 130) with one-piece indicators front and rear to give a low overall profile. This was needed because of a very low bridge on the Leeman Road route in York. Number **238 (FWX813)** had found its way to Scarborough, where it was photographed in Northway outside the Company's premises, in June 1950.

Below: One of the 40 standard L5Gs for the main fleet, No. **262 (JWT290)**. This was a 1950 delivery and was allocated to York depot when new and until 1955. In this view it is at Northway, Scarborough in July 1950, apparently on private hire work, with a similar vehicle parked behind.

Above: When the Construction & Use Regulations were amended to allow legal operation of 8ft-wide by 30ft-long PSVs, some unusual compromise vehicles appeared in the interim period before manufacturers were geared to produce new designs. West Yorkshire's No. **SGW4 (JYG719)** - which had been No. 425 when new in 1951 - was a Bristol LL5G 7ft 6ins-wide by 30ft-long chassis fitted with an 8ft-wide body seating 39. The overhang of the body is very evident in this August 1957 picture at Northway, Scarborough.

Below: Twelve Bristol LWL6Gs - a true 8ft x 30ft chassis - with Eastern Coach Works fully fronted 35-seat coach bodies entered service in 1951. Widely known among enthusiasts as "Queen Marys", these coaches performed a wide variety of duties. In this Nottingham view in August 1951, No. **671 (JYG749)** was working on hire to Associated Motorways with "Leeds" as its advertised destination.

<<< Previous page: Number **714** (**EWY403**) was a 1946 ECW-bodied lowbridge 55-seater on the Bristol K5G chassis. There were three for the main fleet, three for Keighley-West Yorkshire and three highbridge examples delivered that year - the first postwar double-deckers. All featured front, rear and side destination screens and the lowbridge examples had only one cream relief band. Number 714 was a Leeds depot allocation all its life and was photographed at Vicar Lane bus station, Leeds in August 1949, after the side indicator screen had been panelled over but before the addition (in March 1951) of a cream band below the upper-deck windows.

This page: The more powerful six-cylinder Bristol-engined K6B was the standard from 1947. These two examples at Vicar Lane bus station in August 1949 show the side indicators painted out - an interim measure until they were permanently panelled over. Neither bus is exactly identifiable although the upper is one of 728 - 737 (FWX 821 - 830)

Later Bristol Lodekkas were of the redesigned and facelifted FS6B type. Apart from one FS6B, all West Yorkshire's Lodekkas were of rear-entrance layout, and even the single front-entrance exception was later exchanged with United Automobile Services Ltd for a rear-entrance vehicle. KDX136 onwards featured the redesigned radiator grille and offset front registration-number plate as well as "T" destination display at front and rear. **YDX149 (147CWR)** entered service in December 1962 and in this view *(above)* at Scarborough in July 1963 had been fitted with grilles over the Cave-Browne-Cave air intakes. **956BWR** *(below)* was delivered in 1962 as fleet number KDX142. It was renumbered 2742 in the October 1971 scheme and on the winding up of Keighley-West Yorkshire in 1975 was further renumbered as **1742**. Wearing NBC corporate livery of poppy-red with one white band, it is seen on loan to the Trent Motor Traction Company at Derby in July 1976.

EUG1 (LWR431), delivered in 1953, had a 41-seat dual purpose body by Eastern Coach Works. It was the first of 68 Bristol LS5G integrally constructed single-deckers delivered between then and the end of 1957. Unlike its northerly neighbour, United, West Yorkshire never ordered the LS with service-bus seating. EUG1, pictured in July 1953 at Scarborough, was on the Bradford express service. At that time it was a Bradford allocation but in October 1953 it moved to Leeds.

Above: In December 1954, **EUG1** was equipped with Cave-Browne-Cave heating with the air intake in the front dome. This meant that the destination indicator had to be resited below the front windscreen. In November 1956 it was reseated as a 45-seat service bus and spent the next 12 years as a Pateley Bridge depot allocation. In July 1968 it was at Harrogate bus station at the head of a line of West Yorkshire single-deckers.

Below: Fleet number **EUG30** (**OWX142**) was a 1955 vehicle which, despite being renumbered SUG30 (suggesting service bus status) in March 1959, retained its more comfortable, high-backed "dual-purpose" seats throughout its life in the West Yorkshire fleet. There are variations in livery treatment when EUG30 is compared with EUG1 above. The vehicle was a Leeds allocation when photographed at Derby bus station in May 1959.

Twenty Bristol LS6G coaches with 39-seat Eastern Coach Works bodies entered service between 1952 and 1955. **CUG14 (MWY620)** was new in June 1954 to Harrogate depot, moving in May 1958 to Keighley. It was at Grantham Old Bus Station in March 1955.

WEST YORKSHIRE

Above: **CUG4 (LWR409)** was one of the pilot batch of LS6G coaches, new in 1952, which featured the original Eastern Coach Works body design, with one-piece windscreens, for 30ft-long coaches. The coach was some five years old when caught by the photographer inside Northway garage, Scarborough in June 1957.

Below: The final batch of coaches in West Yorkshire's CUG class was a trio of Bristol MW6Gs with Eastern Coach Works 39-seat bodies which entered service in March 1967. The origin of this body shape was a "breaking the mould" exercise on ECW's part which moved emphatically away from the Lowestoft coachbuilder's traditional coaching bodies. These three 1967 coaches were for several years the mainstay of the Low Harrogate Excursions. **CUG46 (NWW735E)** was at Westwood coach park, Scarborough in June 1971.

That mould-breaking design appeared in the West Yorkshire fleet in April 1962 when CUG33-35 were delivered. When new they carried the cream and maroon coaching livery. The change to NBC corporate white did nothing to enhance the lines of the coachwork. Renumbered 1074 (9169YG), pictured at Harrogate bus station in March 1975, had been fitted with a new offside destination blind which contained mainly route numbers for National Express workings. The 1954 numbering scheme with prefix letters was replaced in October 1971 by an all-number system because of the introduction of computerised record-keeping.

Above: Bristol MW6G No. **1136 (836BWY)** was new in July 1963 as fleet number SMG28. These were the only single-deckers with "T" destination indicators in the West Yorkshire fleet. The 41ins. destination screen had been blanked off at each end to permit the use of a 30ins. blind as used on all other contemporary single-deckers. The bus was working a Sunday version of one of the Harrogate local services in April 1973.

Below: The mid-sixties saw the widespread introduction into Tilling fleets of 36ft-long Bristol RE single-deckers offering ten or so more seats than had been available in the 30ft MW. This one, West Yorkshire's **1213 (HWT572C)**, was a 54-seater which entered service with the fleet number SRG13 in August 1965 as an Ilkley allocation for the long 76 service from Skipton to Tadcaster. By the time of this April 1973 view it was at Harrogate depot where it was primarily employed on crew-operated local services.

Above: Odd man out among the 33 Bristol RELL6Gs (low-floor version with Gardner engine) delivered between 1964 and 1966 was fleet number **1223** (**MWX140D**), new in November 1966 as SRG23. It featured dual doors and semi-automatic transmission. It was exhibited in the demonstration park at the 1966 Commercial Motor Show. Inside the show was another dual-door RE, R61 (KHN761D) of United Automobile Services Ltd. Whereas the United example was rebuilt to single-door specification before going into service, the West Yorkshire vehicle retained its original layout, as seen in this Harrogate bus station view of March 1979.

Below: Fleet number **1032** (**CWY499H**) was a 1970 47-seat Bristol RELH6L (a high-floorline version for coaching duties fitted with a Leyland engine). In its 13-year life with West Yorkshire it carried no fewer than five fleet numbers: CRG18 on delivery from ECW (it had been intended that it would have a Gardner engine), CRL2 before entering service, 1032 in the October 1971 fleet renumbering, 2302 in the November 1978 coach and dual-purpose renumbering scheme and finally 2520 in September 1979. It was photographed at Nottingham, Victoria in June 1972, carrying cream and maroon livery which it lost in September 1972 in favour of National all-over white.

The first Bristol RE coaches had been 11 RELH6Gs with Eastern Coach Works dual-purpose 47-seat bodies. These vehicles were effectively coaches, the power-operated folding doors conferring the "dual-purpose" status. At around this time the distinction between "coach" and "dual-purpose" became somewhat blurred: United's extremely comfortable RE class, for example, had only 43 well-spaced seats as well also as driver-controlled power doors. West Yorkshire's **1007 (LWT369D)** *(above)* was new in April 1966 as ERG7. It was later painted in NBC poppy-red and white "local coach" livery, then into National white and finally reverted to poppy-red and white. It was at Southgate Street, Leicester in April 1972. Number **1029 (YYG541G)**, another 47-seater, was classified as "coach" rather "dual-purpose" because of its slam-type door. It was new in November 1969 as fleet number CRG13 and was one of the RELH6Gs later rebuilt by Willowbrook. In this July 1972 view at Woodthorpe, Nottingham 1029 heads a convoy which included a Yorkshire Woollen Leyland Leopard, another West Yorkshire RELH and a Nottingham Corporation double-decker

In 1977/78 seven West Yorkshire RELH6Gs were rebuilt by Willowbrook and equipped for driver-only operation. The resulting hybrids had a distinctive, if scarcely attractive, appearance which was unique to West Yorkshire. Number **2517 (YYG540G)**, thus rebuilt, is contrasted with the original styling as seen on No. **1015** **(PWR858E)** alongside, in a Wellington Street, Leeds view *(above)* dating from September 1978. The visual oddness of the ECW/Willowbrook hybrids is emphasised *(below)* in a picture of No. **2517** taken at Harrogate in March 1979. The Willowbrook rebuilds were used on National Express workings as well as stage-carriage duties, the latter exemplified by 2517 on service 36 to Leeds. Number **1015** appears again *(>>> opposite page)* in National white colours. Despite the livery, the clean, harmonious lines of the original Eastern Coach Works design are evident. The photograph was taken at Harrogate bus station in April 1973. Number 1015 had been new in April 1967 as CRG2. It became 2504 in the dual-purpose series in October 1978 for the last few months of its life, although it retained the white coaching livery throughout its remaining time with West Yorkshire.

<<< Opposite page: A surprise purchase in 1977 was of six second-hand Bedford coaches from the Trent Motor Traction Company Limited. Number **1089 (ERB343H)**, seen at Park Parade, Harrogate opposite the Company's Conductor Training School, in September 1978, was a 1970 VAM70 with Duple 41-seat coachwork. Number 1090 was a similar machine and the other four were YRQs with Plaxton bodies. All six had been new to Midland General before passing to Trent.

Above: The Company was privatised in 1987 and the first full-sized new vehicles subsequently purchased were two 49-seat Leyland Lynxes. They introduced a new, mainly cream, livery and fleetname style. Number **1202 (E325SWY)** was at Harrogate bus station in May 1988.

Below: The last new full-sized vehicles bought before privatisation were 11 double-deck coaches of Neoplan or MCW Metroliner construction and two Duple-bodied Leyland Tigers. Number **2007 (C756CWX)**, in National Express livery at Victoria coach station, London in June 1986, was one of the Metroliners. They had a short life with West Yorkshire and were withdrawn in 1989 when the Company ceased National Express work.

Above: The Duple-bodied Leyland Tigers had probably the most exotic appearance of any ever owned by the Company. Both entered service in National Holidays livery, 2414 later receiving National Express lettering whilst 2145 was repainted in "Northern Rose" livery. Number **2414** (**C63CYG**) was at Nottingham, Victoria in December 1986 on a service to Birmingham.

Below: "Northern Rose" was introduced as a fleetname for the Company's coaching operation in 1986. A proportion of the coaching fleet received an appropriate livery in two shades of blue and white, as seen on Leyland Tiger **2711** (**B83SWX**).

Sixty-three Leyland Olympians entered service between 1983 and 1985. Numbers **1814 (FUM489Y)** *(above)* and **1829 (A94KWW)** *(below)* both entered service in 1983 and are seen in Harrogate respectively in May and October of that year. 1814 was later converted by Optare to dual-purpose seating and reliveried as shown by No. 1842 on page 64. Number 1829 was one of four originally ordered for the York-West Yorkshire fleet. The Olympian, effectively a Bristol design, was widely regarded as the successor to the Bristol VR. Number 1814 was built at Bristol and was one of the very last chassis to emerge from the Brislington factory before it was closed down by British Leyland.

Ten Leyland Olympians were converted by Optare to dual-purpose 70-seaters and were repainted in an attractive red and cream livery. They were put to use generally on inter-urban services in an attempt to improve passenger loadings through enhanced levels of comfort - the brave new world of deregulation and privatisation. Number **1842 (A605NYG)** stars in this Harrogate bus station scene of May 1988. The Leyland Lynx in the background is No. **1201 (E324SWY)**.

THE WEST YORKSHIRE INFORMATION SERVICE

If you have enjoyed this book and would like to know more about the West Yorkshire Road Car Company Limited and its successors, you might be interested in joining the West Yorkshire Information Service. The WYIS was formed in 1951 and from the outset good relations were established with the Company, making it possible to produce a comprehensive monthly news bulletin. The WYIS thrives to this day and its bulletin covers the activities of Keighley & District, Harrogate & District, First York and Yorkshire Coastliner. Articles relating to the history of West Yorkshire and the current whereabouts of ex-West Yorkshire vehicles are also included.

Membership details can be obtained by contacting Mr J F Gill, Hon. Secretary WYIS, 8 Ash Bank Road, Ripon, North Yorkshire, HG4 2EQ.